The Buildings
of Bath

The Buildings of Bath

RICHARD K. MORRISS

With photographs by Ken Hoverd

ALAN SUTTON

First published in the United Kingdom in 1993 by
Alan Sutton Publishing Limited
Phoenix Mill · Far Thrupp · Stroud · Gloucestershire

First published in the United States of America in 1993 by
Alan Sutton Publishing Inc. · 83 Washington Street · Dover NH 03820

British Library Cataloguing in Publication Data

Morriss, Richard K.
  1. Buildings of Bath
  I. Title
  720.942398
  ISBN 0–7509–0256–6

Library of Congress Cataloging in Publication Data applied for

*Cover illustrations: front: detail of Wood the Elder's Circus, his last work. He did not live to see
it finished and the work was continued by his son; inset: the focal point of Great Pulteney
Street, the former Sydney Hotel, originally built by Charles Harcourt Masters in 1796; Back:
the Palladian bridge in the grounds of Prior Park, Ralph Allen's country mansion, is a close
copy of the one at Wilton and was built by Richard Jones in about 1755.*

Typeset in 11/14 Times
Typesetting and origination by
Alan Sutton Publishing Limited.
Printed in Great Britain by
Redwood Books, Trowbridge, Wiltshire

Contents

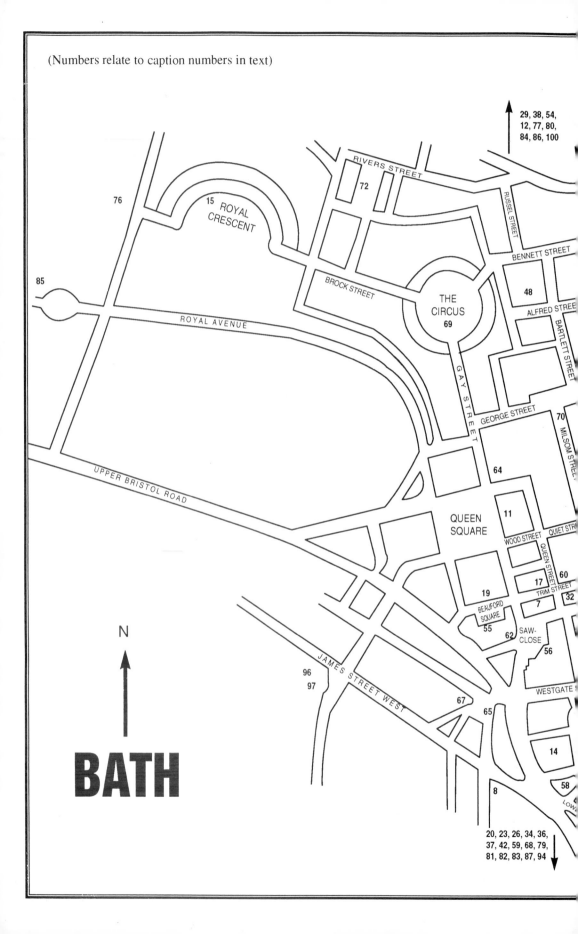

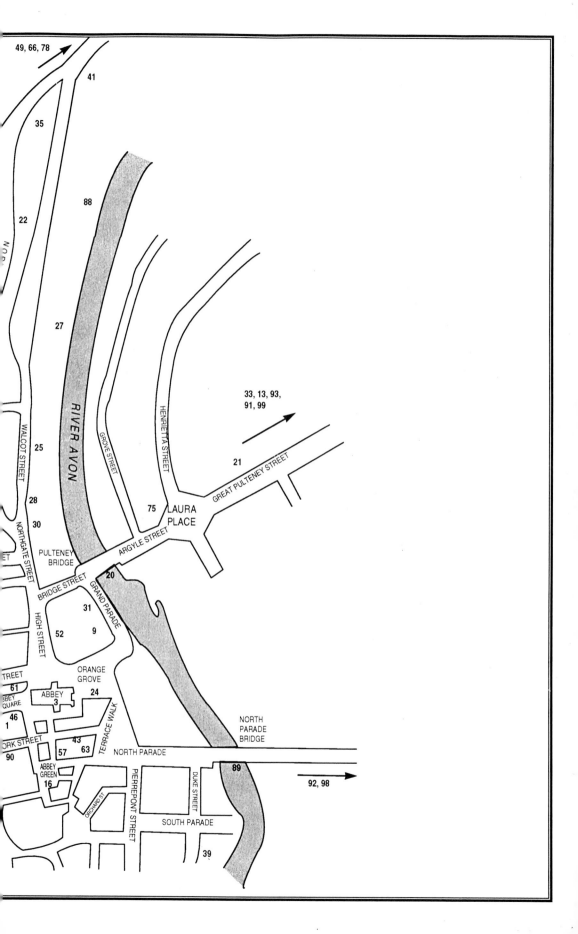

Introduction

The city of Bath, one of the oldest in Britain, owes its existence
to its famous hot springs. Tradition says it was founded by
Bladud, a prince reduced to herding swine after contracting lep-
rosy and being exiled. The pigs caught his disease but, wallow-
ing in warm marshes by the Avon, were miraculously cured.
Bladud jumped in after them, was also cured, returned home,
became king and built a city at the healing springs. This is just a
legend, but there was probably some sort of settlement, possibly
religious, at Bath before the Roman conquest.

By the end of the first century AD the Roman settlement of
Aquae Sulis was the home of an important healing cult. The
Romans had combined the local Celtic deity, Sul, with their
goddess Minerva to create Sulis Minerva, the new goddess who
presided over the springs. They also created a sophisticated
supply system to channel the hot waters into a huge Great Bath.
Alongside were a series of temples and bath-houses, and around
the complex grew a small town that relied on religion, healing
and recreation. For over three centuries the town flourished and
enjoyed a Europe-wide reputation until, at the start of the fifth
century, the legions were recalled to Italy. Aquae Sulis, together
with the rest of the British province, was abandoned.

The Dark Ages that followed are now known to have been far
less barbarous than once thought. However, the post-Roman
society was a rural one and most of the Roman towns were gradually abandoned. Bath's proud civic buildings crumbled away
and an eighth-century poem, 'The Ruin', lamented that its *enta
geweore*, or 'wondrous walls', were grey with lichen, the towers
were ruinous and the roofs all fallen. The water system broke
down and the area again became marshy, with successive flood
deposits burying the old city beneath layers of mud. Some life
survived within the comparative safety of the Roman walls, and

1 The huge Roman Great Bath was only rediscovered in the 1880s, but was then restored and displayed. Unfortunately, the sheets of Mendip lead that once lined it were removed at the same time. The columns supporting the roof had to be strengthened when a vault was added in the third century. Most of the work above the their bases is Victorian.

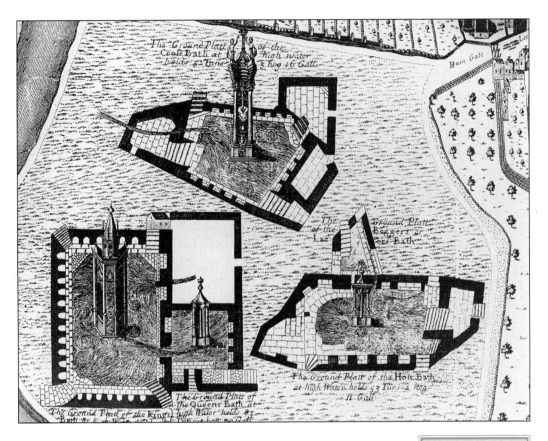

2 Details of the main
baths, King's, Queen's,
Cross and Hot Baths, as
they appeared in a detail
of Gilmore's map of
1694.

the hot springs may have retained their reputation for healing, as
well as their religious importance.

Bath was considered to be a city in AD 577 when the *Anglo-
Saxon Chronicle* recorded that Bathanceaster, Gloucester and
Cirencester fell to the Saxons after a decisive battle at Dyrham, a
few miles to the north. By the seventh century Bath was in
Hwicce, a sub-kingdom of Mercia, and at the end of the next century was described as a 'celebrated town' with a 'most famous'
monastery. In the late ninth century Hwicce came under the control
of Alfred the Great's expanding Wessex. Alfred re-established
urban life in English society and Bath benefited. Its old Roman
defences were rebuilt, the streets may have been realigned, a mint
was established and in 901 the ruling council, or witan, met there.
On Whit Sunday 973 Edgar, King of all England, was crowned in
the monastery church of St Peter. The Saxon revival ended in the

3

early eleventh century and in 1013 the thegns of western England surrendered to the Danish king, Swein, at Bath.

Just over fifty years later the Normans conquered and then, in 1088, fought among themselves. A plot to put William II's brother, Robert of Normandy, on the English throne was put down, but not until Bath, mostly owned by the king, had been ravaged by the rebels. Bade was then a sizeable town of about a thousand people. In 1090 the new Bishop of Wells, John de Villula, moved his cathedra, or bishop's chair, to the monastery church at Bath. He then bought William's share of the city and for nearly 450 years the church controlled its affairs. John de Villula rebuilt the city and started to construct a new cathedral. As he was a physician, he may also have been responsible for bringing the hot springs back to national prominence. According to the twelfth-century *Gesta Stephani*, the healing properties of Bath's springs were known throughout Europe. In 1218 a later bishop returned to Wells, which became the seat of the diocese of Bath and Wells. The abbey church in Bath ceased to be a cathedral, becoming instead a priory church for the monastery.

The absence of a bishop, and the rather sorry succession of priors left to run the town's affairs, led to a gentle run-down of the religious buildings and baths. In the fourteenth century the town, with many others in Somerset, became an important weaving centre using the wool from local flocks. One of the Chaucer's story-telling pilgrims in his *Canterbury Tales* was a 'good wif . . . of biside BATHE' who excelled at 'clooth-mayking'. Bath had also become a regional market and, in many ways, the baths were just a sideline, although an important one, in what was otherwise a typical West Country town.

At the end of the fifteenth century the Norman cathedral was virtually in ruins, and in 1499 Bishop King decided to build a new one. The city itself seems to have benefited from the attention given to it by this bishop, and when John Leland visited in 1536 he wrote:

The city of Bath is set both in a fruitful and pleasant bottom, which is environed on every side with great hills, out of which come many springs of pure water that be conveyed by divers ways to serve the city, many houses in the town having pipes of lead to convey water from place to place.

3 A general view of the Abbey Square, with the recently restored west front of Bath Abbey in the background and Brydon's Concert Room extension (1896) to the Pump Room to the right.

Leland also described Bishop King's church, still not quite finished then or when the monastery was dissolved in 1539. Most of its land ended up in private hands, but the baths remained Crown property before being given to the Corporation in 1552. Ten years later the first of many books praising the healing powers of the waters was published by William Turner, Dean of Wells. The Corporation, after neglecting the baths, now saw the potential for a regular income and restored them. Bath gradually became a fashionable healing resort, patronized by the aristocracy. The Earl of Salisbury, for example, came in 1612 and was 'exceedingly revived by the Bath'. Sadly his cure was short-lived – he died three weeks later. In 1613 James I's queen, Anne of Denmark, came. The fact that she did so again two years later no doubt enhanced Bath's reputation, and in 1634 a visitor commented on 'those admired unparalleled, medicinal, sulphorous hot bathes'.

In the Civil War (1642–9), Bath wisely switched its allegiance several times between Crown and Parliament. It had no great strategic value for either side, so suffered very little apart from the drop in numbers of those using the baths. In the late seventeenth century the town still retained its medieval street pattern and was mainly confined within the old town walls. In 1654 the diarist John Evelyn described its streets as 'uneven, narrow and unpleasant'. Samuel Pepys, who visited in 1668, also commented on the narrow streets, but found the 'town most of stone, and clean', with some 'very fair stone houses'. To the redoubtable Celia Fiennes in the 1680s, 'the baths in my opinion . . . [made] the town unpleasant, the air thick and hot'. Celia unconsciously noted the beginnings of an important change when she commented on the 'several good houses built for lodgings that are new and adorned with good furniture'. After several decades in the doldrums, Bath's reputation was reviving. In 1702 Queen Anne visited Bath, giving it the royal seal of approval again. In the century that followed, a virtually new city swept away the old, and a fairly ordinary town in rural Somerset of about two thousand souls became the fashionable capital of England.

Queen Anne's visit was by no means the only reason for Bath's transformation. It coincided with the growth of high society gambling, and Bath, far enough away from London, well known to the gentry and again enjoying royal patronage, was a

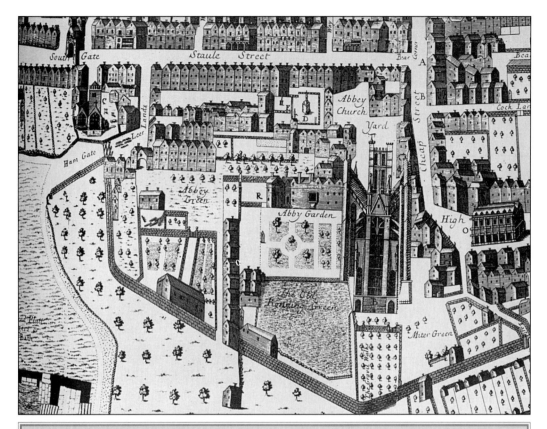

4 An extract from an illustrated map of 1692–4 by Joseph Gilmore shows the central area of the city, still very much medieval in appearance, just before it was swept away by the Georgians.

suitable place to lose money. This would probably have been a short-term trend had it not been for three remarkable men who happened to be in Bath during the same period.

The first was a Welshman, Richard 'Beau' Nash. He had failed at university, in the Army and at Law. Surviving as a gambler in London, he saw potential in Bath and became its master of ceremonies in 1705. Presiding over the town's chaotic social life, he set down a rigid set of rules and regulations and, astonishingly, they were obeyed. The Bath 'season' he created became a regular event on the fashionable calendar. It was later said of this uncrowned 'King of Bath' that 'by the Force of Genius he erected the City of Bath into a Province of Pleasure'.

Bathing in and drinking the waters were still supposedly the reasons for going to Bath, but more and more people came simply for recreation. According to Defoe, writing in the 1720s, it

5 The best views of Bath are from the hillside above Widcombe or, as here, from Claverton Down.

had become 'the resort of the sound rather than the sick; the bathing is made more a sport and diversion than a physical prescription for health; and the town is taken up raffling, gaming, visiting and, in a word, all sorts of gallantry and levity'.

The increasing popularity led, inevitably, to growth and a need for new housing, which in turn led to a building boom. The local raw material was stone and most of the stone quarries were soon in the hands of Ralph Allen, a man of obscure Cornish origins. Allen had already made one fortune after arriving in Bath by reorganizing the national postal system. He proceeded to make a second out of the quarries on Combe Down, just south of the city.

Initially the new houses were built in much the same haphazard way as before, though the style of individual houses was certainly more up to date. In 1724 the antiquary William Stukeley thought Bath 'handsomely built', but 'The small compass of the city has made the inhabitants croud up the streets to an unseemingly and inconvenient narrowness'. This was all to change with the return to his native city in 1727 of a young, confident architect, John Wood. Wood was also something of an eccentric and a self-styled, but extremely bad, antiquary. He dreamed of a new Bath, of wide streets, squares and open spaces, and of restoring the lost grandeur of the Romans. The old was to be swept away by the antique, so that the city would 'appear much the same as Virgil declares Carthage to have appeared to Aeneas'. Only a fraction of Wood's vision was ever realized, but the basic principles he laid down were more or less followed for the next hundred years.

Bath remained sufficiently fashionable and prosperous to allow itself to be rebuilt in this way. The rich, the famous, the hopeful and the hangers-on all flocked to the city in the season and enjoyed the social whirl of the assembly rooms, the parties, the concerts, the promenading, the gambling and the political intrigue of the coffee-houses. If Bath were to fix blue plaques for every famous writer, artist or politician that spent time in the city during the eighteenth century, there would hardly be a house left untouched; it was virtually the second capital.

Bath's expansion came to a temporary stop in 1793 when the whole country suffered a financial crisis. Several banks in Bath folded and ruined some of the biggest builders and architects in the process. Others were unable to carry on because of the economic uncertainties of the Napoleonic Wars. Terraces and squares were left unfinished and empty until stability returned at the end of the 1810s. By this time sea-bathing was becoming more popular, helped in the 1840s by the newly built railways. Just as suddenly as Bath had become fashionable it stopped being so and most of the grand new housing schemes were abandoned. Attempts to revive the town's reputation as a major medicinal spa town by improving the baths had limited success. Even the Arts suffered. Bath had been renowned for its music, but by 1839 only 'the mere semblance of an orchestra remained . . . to scrape upon a few sorry cremonas the same eternal bars of Corelli and Handel every day at two o'clock'.

Ironically the city was by no means in decline – far from it. Between 1801 and 1841 the population grew from around thirty-three thousand to over fifty thousand. Indeed, the fairly rapid

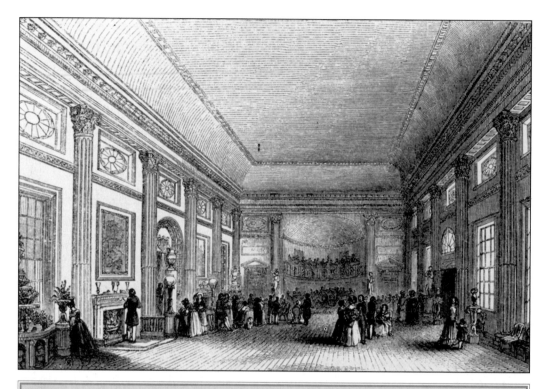

6 By the mid-nineteenth century the elegance of the Great Pump Room was beginning to fade as Bath was no longer the fashionable place it had been. This print dates to about 1850.

growth of Bath during the mid- and late nineteenth century may have also contributed to the loss of its fashionable status. It was developing as a fairly ordinary city with typical Victorian middle-class suburbs of detached and semi-detached villas, and working-class areas of terraced houses closer to the industries that provided much of the employment. Although its fashionable heyday was gone, Bath still attracted visitors by projecting itself as a quiet inland resort, relying on the quality of its Georgian architecture and the reputation given to it by writers such as Jane Austen. Many people retired to Bath and, due in no small part to this, that architectural heritage was preserved, largely untouched, until the middle of the twentieth century.

During the Second World War Bath was seen as a safe place for both evacuees and government offices, but the city's tranquillity was shattered in a few terrifying hours during one spring

night in 1942. That March the RAF had attacked the historic
north German cities of Lübeck and Rostock. In retaliation the
Luftwaffe began the infamous Baedeker raids on 'cultural' tar-
gets. The second hit Bath on 24 April. On that dreadful night
over four hundred people were killed and many buildings were
damaged or destroyed. The horror and obscenity of war had
come to the town whose very architecture expressed the age of
enlightenment, the age of reason.

After the war the slow process of rebuilding the city began.
Where possible, damaged buildings were repaired or rebuilt as
carefully as possible. It is sometimes difficult to believe that the
Assembly Rooms, parts of the Royal Crescent and much of
Somerset Place are all post-war reconstructions. Only a few
buildings still bear the scars of war and stand as testimony to
man's inhumanity to man. Buildings beyond repair had to be

8 Most of the damage inflicted on Bath by the bombs of April 1942 has been repaired and the horror mostly forgotten. This pockmarked remnant of a once-fine Georgian terrace in James Street West is an important reminder of the brutality of war.

demolished, but slowly the city was restored. Unfortunately the slow progress came to a shuddering halt in the 1960s – the real Dark Ages of urban planning.

Bath is now a thriving city with a population of eighty thousand. It is an important commercial centre for the region and has a surprising amount of industry. Above all, it is one of the main tourist attractions in England. Visitors come from all over the world, not to take the waters or mix with high society but to enjoy the rich architectural heritage of a bygone age and to walk in the footsteps of the famous. The only surviving link with the medicinal hot springs is the Royal Mineral Water Hospital for Rheumatic Diseases, begun as the General Hospital in the 1730s thanks to the efforts of, among others, that remarkable triumvirate, Nash, Allen and Wood.

9 C.E. Davis's Empire Hotel, it has to be said, is a monstrosity. Stylistically bizarre and far too big for its prominent position between the abbey and the river, it is a prime example of Edwardian bad taste. It was built between 1899 and 1902, but ceased to be an hotel in the Second World War when it was taken over for military purposes. In the foreground, appropriately, is a monument to Edward VII.

Left to right: **10** This doorway is in Belmont, built around 1770. The architect is unknown; **11** One of the elder Wood's more elaborate doorway designs is in the east terrace of Queen Square; **12** A detail of a doorway in Camden Crescent. The elephant in the keystone is part of the Marquis of Camden's crest; **13** A detail of a doorway in Pinch's New Sydney Place, showing the simple but refined neo-classicism that is typical of his work. The elegant lamp-holder is known as a 'throwover'.

Architectural
Character

Bath is unique. It is, without doubt, the finest Georgian city in Britain and one of the most elegant in Europe. Few cities can boast such harmony of style, scale and texture, and, in Britain, only the New Town suburb of Edinburgh comes anywhere near. It is not simply that most of Bath was built in a single century in the beautiful local freestone, and to the pervading architectural fashion of the day; what makes Bath unique is that it was constructed on a grand scale. Wood's ambitious new city might never have been completed, but fortunately the architects and speculators that followed him all developed their own areas of the city in the same grand manner – as squares and parades, or crescents and palatial terraces. Monotony was prevented by the steep slopes of the Avon Valley, good planning and luck.

The local stone came from the hills around the city, notably from Combe and Bathampton Downs. It is an oolitic limestone, varying greatly in quality depending on the strata from which it has been taken. Its main advantage is that it is a freestone, that is a stone that can be cut in any direction rather than just along the bedding. This makes it very easy to fashion into smooth, ashlar blocks, and amenable to delicate carving, which meant that even the most humble buildings could be decorated in a way seldom seen in other parts of Britain. On the other hand, the stone is rather porous and its pale honey colour can quickly become dis-coloured by soot pollution. This is one reason why the stone failed to gain a foothold in London.

Despite the ease with which the stone could be cut, the earliest buildings were built of roughly coursed stone. Even when the

14 Chapel Court has some remarkable, unaltered houses of the early years of the eighteenth century. The stone is good quality ashlar, the mouldings classical and the symmetry obvious. Only the archaic dormer gables defy the new architectural fashions of the day.

15 This unusual view of the Royal Crescent clearly shows that, in Bath, the fronts of the houses were far more important than the backs. The west end of the crescent is part of the magnificent stone sweep overlooking the city, articulated by attached Ionic columns and finished in ashlar. The houses behind were built by different builders and to different requirements, resulting in total, but fascinating, disharmony.

16 Abbey Green is traditionally the site of the monks' bowling green. It is now a pleasant open space surrounded by houses of several different dates. The latest addition is St Michael's Arch. The name stems not from religion, but from the brand name of the well-known department store that built it in 1973.

elegantly ashlared Georgian terraces were constructed, their rear walls were often of this much poorer quality masonry. The 'backsides' of Bath's houses are very revealing and, in some ways, more interesting than their public façades. No other building material seems to have been used to any great extent in the city: there are no surviving timber-framed houses and little evidence that there were ever any. Brick, fashionable when Bath was so popular, is mainly restricted to a few later nineteenth-century terraces on the outskirts of the town. Even the modern buildings of concrete, steel and glass have, by an Act of 1925, had to be clad with Bath stone or a suitable substitute.

Most of the earlier buildings were swept away in the great Georgian rebuilding, so only a few survive. At the end of the seventeenth century these would have been little different from those of any other small West Country town. Details still included mullioned windows and Cotswold gables. Even when more sophisticated architecture arrived at the start of the eighteenth century, it came from London or Bristol. With the return of Wood, however the roles were reversed and everywhere else copied Bath.

Wood was, in many respects, a fanatic, but one that managed to combine the fanatic's single-mindedness with innate architectural skill and a splendid eye for townscape. Just as Beau Nash transformed Bath's chaotic social life, Wood did the same for the city's diverse architecture. Nash laid down a strict code of etiquette, just as Wood employed the architectural rules known as Palladianism.

Palladianism was based on the writings of a provincial Italian architect, Andrea Palladio (1508–80), specifically his *Four Books of Architecture*. Palladio had studied Vitruvius, the author of the only Roman work on architecture to survive, and had visited and surveyed many of the ruined buildings of the Empire. According to Palladio, all beauty stemmed from proportion, and the best proportions had already been discovered by the Romans and developed as their 'orders'. These orders are best recognized by the tops, or capitals, of the columns used so frequently in classical architecture. The three main orders were the plain but sturdy Doric; the more ornate Ionic (with its ram's horns); and the ornate, leafy Corinthian.

Inigo Jones introduced Palladianism into England at the start of the seventeenth century, but it didn't catch on. After the Restoration in 1660, French and Flemish influences were more important and, for grand houses in particular, the somewhat florid Baroque style was popular. In a reaction against these trends, Palladianism was finally accepted as a result of the efforts of the Duke of Burlington and the architect Colen Campbell in the early eighteenth century. Based on the discipline of Rome it was, as far as Wood was concerned, ideal. As it was being used in the grandest of aristocractic country houses, it was the height of fashion, and considered eminently suitable for the city in which the upper classes spent several months each year.

Having been applied rather naïvely to individual buildings, Palladianism was already known in Bath before Wood. However, he took the basic Palladian rules and applied them to whole streetscapes. In his *Essay towards a Description of Bath*, Wood

17 Queen Street, seen here through Trim Bridge (also called St John's Gate), was one of the earlier developments outside the old city and lacks the uniformity of much of eighteenth-century Bath. The sets in the road surface are a welcome feature, but it really is a shame about the double yellow lines.

claimed to have first thought of rebuilding Bath in 1725 when working in Yorkshire. He put forward housing schemes that would be based around three key open spaces: the 'Royal Forum of Bath'; the 'Grand Circus', which was to be 'for the exhibition of Sports'; and the 'Imperial Gymnasium', for 'the Practise of medicinal Exercises'. Only a fragment of the huge Forum project was built, the North and South Parades, and nothing at all of the mysterious Gymnasium. Wood only laid the foundation stone for the Circus shortly before his death, but it stands as one of the most adventurous pieces of English townscape.

Wood's ideas were not entirely original. His first major scheme, Queen Square, owed much to an unbuilt scheme of Shepherd's for Grosvenor Square in London. The basic principle of large-scale, uniform developments quickly caught on in Bath, but was generally carried out with less success. Among the earlier

18 John Wood's Queen Square revolutionized high-class urban development in Britain. It was the first successful attempt at a single, cohesive plan for an individual square, using the north side as the focal point. Designed as a palace, it actually contained several different houses and was flanked by lesser buildings on the three other sides of the square.

19 Beauford Square was an early example of uniform urban planning, laid out by Strahan soon after Wood had started his Queen Square project at the end of the 1720s. The scale, however, is fairly humble and there is no sense of the dramatic.

imitators, though on a more modest scale, was John Strahan, a Bristol architect. Initially the new developments took place mainly in an area known as the New, or Upper, Town, on the northern slopes overlooking the old city, and in the low-lying region by the river to the west. The Bath Improvement Act of 1789 allowed greater redevelopment within the walls.

Wood died in 1754 and only saw part of his grand scheme completed. His son, John Wood the Younger, every bit as good an architect as his father, helped to perpetuate Palladianism in Bath for the rest of the century. By the latter decades the less-rigid neo-classicism of Robert Adam was becoming very influential. Owing in no small measure to his work, the robust severity of Palladianism gradually gave way to more delicate and sophisticated decoration. Adam designed a complete new development south of the river at Bathwick in the late 1760s, but only his

21 The long, straight vista of Great Pulteney Street, seen here from the fountain in Laura Place, was designed by Thomas Baldwin. It was the axis of a large but unfinished project to develop the area, badly hit by the financial crisis of 1793. In many ways the terraces lining the street are somewhat lacking in character, and the decoration too sparse and too subtle for its scale.

22 The Paragon was designed and built by Thomas Warr Atwood who leased the land in 1768. The curving terrace is conventional plain Palladian, but well executed and finely detailed. The site is steeply sloping and drops away sharply to Walcot Road, so that the basements of the front become full-height ground floors at the rear.

celebrated Pulteney Bridge was ever completed.

The best of the late eighteenth-century architects working in the city was probably Thomas Baldwin. Influenced by Adam, yet still treating townscape on the broad scale of Wood, he developed large areas of the city, including that south of Pulteney Bridge. This was not, however, as satisfying as his earlier work. Great Pulteney Street – 1,100 feet long, 100 feet wide and dead straight – lacks any sense of surprise, and the subtle detailing of the blocks of terraces lining it seem to have neither conviction nor impact. Fortunately the rest of this huge scheme was never completed. Other architects of this period include the innovative John Eveleigh, responsible for Camden Crescent, Somerset Place and Northumberland Crescent; John Palmer, who designed Lansdown Crescent and several churches; and, in the early years of the nineteenth century, John Pinch, who built a

23 When the GWR opened its station in 1840 an attempt was made to provide a suitably grand introduction to the city by the building of neo-classical corner buildings on the end of Manvers Street facing it. They may have been designed by H.E. Goodridge and certainly contrast with Brunel's rather unsightly neo-Jacobean station.

24 Orange Grove Buildings probably date to the early eighteenth century, but owe their present appearance to a radical rebuild at the end of the nineteenth century. The basic shape of the gabled roofline was retained by Charles Edward Davis in 1897, but he added elaborate bargeboards to the gables and hoodmoulds to the first-floor windows. His bizarre tower was a warning of what was to come when he designed the Empire Hotel two years later.

series of fairly similar, chaste terraces.

The close of the Georgian period effectively marked the end of the best-quality architecture of Bath. The Victorian period that followed saw a much sloppier mix of revived antique styles – Greek revival, neo-Tudor and neo-Gothic – often carried out with little judgement and less skill. Among the better local architects of the period was Henry Goodridge, who excelled at the neo-classical but whose neo-Gothic work was somewhat suspect. The Victorian buildings were not really bad, just fairly ordinary, and can be seen in any sizeable town. The architecture of Bath had ceased to be special.

At the same time, the Victorians made slight changes to their predecessors' buildings. Masons were kept busy chiselling away the corners of windows to let in more light and often the sills were lowered, thus damaging previously symmetrical façades.

25 The Hilton Hotel, formerly the Beaumont, was built in 1973, but fails to comply with any of the rules of polite architecture.

26 Modern buildings can, at least, try to be positive contributions to cityscape, as do these new offices block near the station.

27 Bath's grander Georgian architecture has been, on the whole, well cared for and protected. Sadly, the houses of the artisans and lower classes have been devastated in the last thirty years or so, and even the few that survive, like this derelict pair in Walcot, are under threat.

Featureless plate glass began to replace the multi-paned Georgian sashes in an annoying process that has continued until the present day. Perfectly good ashlar was painted over or had signs written on it, and unsympathetic extensions were added to fine buildings, including Pulteney Bridge.

On the other hand, the Victorians also softened the Georgian townscape by introducing trees to formerly bare, open spaces. The plane trees often used have been the subject of some controversy in recent years, especially those in the set pieces of Queen Square and the Circus. Clearly they were not part of the original concept, but the people living in the houses nearby no longer come to Bath to see and be seen while promenading, and would risk getting run over if they did so. The inhabitants now demand more privacy, which the trees offer. In any case, the trees are as much a part of the city now as the buildings, and enhance it with

28 Not all of Bath's thoroughfares are elegant. This unsavoury alleyway runs from Northgate Street down to the river.

29 How a tower block, like this one in the Snowhill area off Walcot Road, could ever be allowed in Bath is a mystery. The other housing blocks in this area are 'medium rise', scattered around the estate at random and with copper roofs that glint a distracting green when viewed from the surrounding hillsides.

their ever-changing colour and texture.

The twentieth century has certainly not enhanced the cityscape. It produced few admirable buildings before the Second World War and has added none since. The plain fact is that the architecture of Bath since the 1950s is either mediocre or bad. Low concrete horrors like the bus station (1958), or tall, glass skyscrapers, such as Rosewell Court (1960), simply don't fit. The Hilton Hotel of 1973, just yards upstream of Adam's Pulteney Bridge, has all the grace and elegance of a breeze-block. By law, all new buildings must be clad in Bath stone or a suitable substitute, but this simply makes matters worse. The stone cladding mocks the real thing, and makes poor designs for concrete and glass even less palatable.

Worst of all, just outside the city centre in the Georgian sub-urbs, the neat stone terraces of artisan housing have been largely

30 In the past ten years or so there has been a general reaction against modernism and a harking back to buildings that echo older styles. This was exactly what was happening when Wood was planning to rebuild Bath at the start of the eighteenth century. The modern Podium development on Northgate Street is at least interesting, but why are all the 'classical' details askew and the proportions awry?

flattened. Modern housing includes medium-rise flats and high-density estates of indifferent design, and the whole balance of this unique city has been radically disturbed. Of course Bath has to have new buildings. Any city is organic and cannot afford to be a museum piece, and many of the buildings that were demolished were certainly not up to modern standards. Yet surely it was not beyond the ken of architects and planners to upgrade and adapt most of them to the needs of the late twentieth century and beyond. As for their replacements, there is never any excuse for bad architecture or poor planning. The modern buildings of Bath are neither innovative nor exciting. Too few respect those basic harmonies of style, scale and texture that made Georgian Bath one of the most graceful cities in the world.

Defences

Bath is certainly not noted for its military architecture and has never even had a castle. Yet for 1700 years it was protected by a city wall, albeit one often in a state of disrepair. The Roman wall was still standing in the Saxon period and was probably repaired on King Alfred's orders in the late ninth century. The later medieval wall appears to have been built on the same line and was repaired again during the Civil War. Shortly afterwards, Pepys returned to his lodgings in Bath 'walking round the walls of the City, which are good, and the battlements all whole'.

The walls are shown on Gilmour's map of 1692–4, but with the rapid expansion of the city in the eighteenth century they were simply in the way. The two main city gates, the South and North, were demolished in 1755 followed by the West Gate in 1776. The redundant walls were rapidly plundered for building stone and hard core. Virtually nothing survives of them above ground, although in places their route is reflected by the modern street pattern.

The two fragments of the medieval defences that do survive are not particularly inspiring. The most obvious is a heavily restored portion of battlemented wall in Upper Borough Walls, opposite the old Royal Mineral Water Hospital. This is an enthusiastic Victorian rebuild, of which only the lower courses of rubblestone appear to be medieval. Much less well known, tucked away in a very unsalubrious, dark alleyway running down from the back of the Market to the river, is a surviving arch of the East Gate. This was not a principal gateway of the city, merely a sally-port leading to the former Fish Cross by the river and the mill.

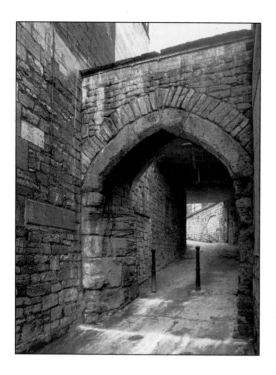

31 Part of the city's medieval East Gate has somehow survived, but is seldom seen. It is tucked away in a rather uninviting and malodorous alleyway between the Market and the back of the Empire Hotel, running down to the Avon.

32 This short section of battlemented wall in Upper Borough Walls is the only fragment remaining of the medieval defences, and most of it, including the parapet, is an enthusiastic Victorian reconstruction.

Churches

The Romans built a small, classical temple to Sulis Minerva in Bath and fragments of its pediment were found when the Pump Room was being built in 1790. The temple was tetrastyle, that is with a pedimented porch supported by four columns. The pediment was decorated with rich carving, the central motif of which is supposedly a Celtic version of the head of Medusa. This Gorgon lady had snakes for hair and a somewhat stony gaze before being defeated by Perseus. The powerful Bath face is certainly not female since it has a beard! In 1909 a full-size replica of the temple was erected in Sydney Gardens, based on the archaeological evidence of the time.

33 The Celtic-Romano version of Sulis Minerva, a powerful, male version of the classical Medusa.

The earliest evidence for Christian worship in Bath is a twelfth-century copy of a charter of 675 by Osric, King of Hwicce, establishing a convent of Holy Virgins. By the eighth century there was a monastery dedicated to St Peter, apparently replacing the convent. The monastery church was rebuilt in stone in the late tenth century and was described by William of Malmesbury as being 'of wondrous workmanship'. Just a few miles to the east is the magnificent late Saxon church of St Laurence's in Bradford-on-Avon, which may give at least some impression of what St Peter's church was like.

The Saxon church was swept away by John de Villula, when he became bishop, in favour of a large and magnificent Norman building. That was, in turn, replaced by the present Abbey church, although a few fragments of it survive within the new fabric. In 1499, Bishop Oliver King, troubled at the state of the church, had dreamed of angels climbing up and down a ladder to heaven and heard a voice saying, 'Let an Olive establish the Crown, and a King restore the Church'. He obviously enjoyed puns and saw this as a clear message. He had been involved in putting Henry VII on the throne, and would now rebuild the

33 In 1909 a copy of the Roman temple to Sulis Minerva was built in Sydney Gardens. It was based on the archaeological evidence known at the time, but does at least give a plausible idea of how the original may have looked.

3 Bath Abbey is one of the few unaltered late-Perpendicular buildings in England, mainly because it was still not finished at the dissolution of its monastery. Started shortly after 1499, it only occupied the nave area of its Norman predecessor. It was built by the Vertue brothers, royal masons who later worked at Windsor Castle.

3 The west front of Bath Abbey depicts, in stone, Bishop King's vision of angels climbing up and down ladders from earth to heaven. The porous Bath stone has meant that most of the original figures are badly worn and many have been replaced. The last renovation finished in 1992.

3 The obelisk east of the abbey was erected in 1734 to celebrate the visit of the Prince of Orange. The surrounding square was also renamed Orange Grove in his honour.

church. The dream is depicted in the splendid stone ladders, complete with angels, on the west front. His love of puns can also be seen in his personal rebus – an olive tree (Oliver), surrounded by a crown (King) and topped by a bishop's mitre – carved into the stonework.

The church is smaller than the Norman one, occupying just the length of its nave. However, King was determined that it would be of the highest quality. A grateful King Henry allowed him to employ the royal master masons, Robert and William Vertue, to design and build the new church. Despite the vagaries of time, demolition contractors and overzealous restorers, Bath Abbey remains one of the few great medieval churches to have been built to its original design, without the distractions of later additions or alterations.

One early change was made by the Vertues themselves and

3 The interior of the abbey is impressive and, unusually for a medieval church, very light and airy. The magnificent fan-vaulting was built in two phases, 350 years apart. This is the oldest, above the chancel, designed by the Vertue brothers.

resulted in the finest feature of the church. It was originally to have trussed timber roofs, but by 1503 elaborate stone fan-vaulting was being used instead. The brothers promised the bishop that 'of the vawte devised for the chancelle . . . there shall be noone so goodely neither in England nor in France', and, until William began St George's Chapel at Windsor Castle a few years later, they were right. After the death of the Vertues the work was carried on by John Molton, master mason to Henry VIII, who supervised the work until it was stopped at the beginning of the Dissolution in 1539.

By that time the church was almost complete, apart from the east window and the fan-vaulting over the nave. The remaining portion of the eastern end of the Norman church was still being taken down. Leland, seeing the tomb of John de Villula, commented that, 'al the church that he made lay to wast, and was onrofid'. After the Dissolution the same fate awaited its replacement. Offered at a price to, but refused by, the citizens of Bath, it was stripped of its lead, glass, iron and even its bells. The bare shell was then given to the city, free, in 1572. Elizabeth I ordered a nationwide collection to be made to finance its restoration and part of it was back in use by 1576. The nave was roofed by Bishop Montague in the early seventeenth century, but the fan-vaulting was only completed as late as 1869 when the abbey was being restored by George Gilbert Scott.

Gilbert Scott's was the second major restoration, the first being carried out by the then city architect, George Philip Masters, in the 1820s and '30s. At that time houses that had been allowed to crowd up against it were demolished. It has been repaired several times since, the last major work, on the west front, being completed in 1992.

The finished abbey has a fairly simple plan, with nave, crossing tower, chancel and transepts. The overall impression inside is of light and height, and the walls seem to comprise nothing but windows. From the outside the grandeur is perhaps marred by the rather narrow crossing tower, and the airy interior perhaps lacks much of the subtle mystery of light and shade seen in earlier medieval churches. Nevertheless, Bath Abbey has avoided the sad fate of so many monastic churches and survives as a fine example of the last phase of English Gothic, the Perpendicular. Of the other monastic buildings, nothing survives above the

3 A detail of the spandrel of the west door of the abbey.

3 St Peter looks down on one side of the west door of the abbey, with St Paul on the other side.

41

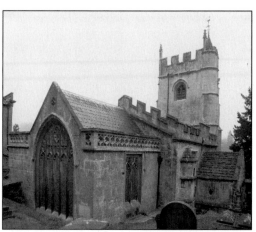

3 The interior of Bath Abbey, looking towards the fine east window, repaired after the damage of 1942.

34 Widcombe Church is dedicated to St Thomas à Becket and, like the abbey, was rebuilt from about 1500 and has seen relatively little alteration since. It is thus one of the last pre-Reformation parish churches to have been built in England. It was either started by, or dedicated to the memory of, Prior Cantlow of Bath.

surface bar a single gate pin embedded in a wall in Abbey Green, said to belong to the Abbey Gateway.

The reason the citizens of Bath were so reluctant to take on the expense of the abbey church was that they already had their own parish churches. There were probably at least four churches before the Norman Conquest within the walls and, soon after, another just to the north. These medieval buildings would have been repaired and rebuilt over the centuries, but nothing remains of them now. The rest of the churches and chapels in Bath are mainly Georgian or Victorian.

Two important exceptions were both connected with one man, Prior Cantlow of Bath, who died at the end of the fifteenth century. Widcombe, lying south of the river, was a totally separate village until the end of the eighteenth century when the expanding city reached it. It retains its manor house and parish

35 The neo-classical church St Swithin's in London Street, Walcot, was designed by John Palmer and built in stages between 1777 and 1790. It was similar in design to Palmer's earlier rebuilding of St James's Church, gutted in the 1942 bombing and pulled down in 1957.

church. The church is dedicated to St Thomas à Becket and, like the abbey, was completely rebuilt at the beginning of the sixteenth century because the old one was 'by its great age obliged to be taken down'. It is not clear if Cantlow built it or if it was erected in his memory. Unlike the abbey, designed by royal masons in the very latest architectural style of the court, St Thomas's is much more local in character. It is a competent and solid example of parish church architecture from the decades immediately before the English Reformation, boasting a battlemented nave, chancel and tower, a rood-stair turret and a fine east window.

A smaller church, St Mary Magdalene in Holloway, was definitely rebuilt by Cantlow, and was once attached to a leper hospital. Probably of Norman origin, work on the new church seems to have begun in 1495, and medieval additions survive despite

36 Eighteenth-century Gothic was whimsical and not meant to be taken too seriously. It is usually known as 'Gothick' to distinguish it from real medieval work or serious imitations. John Pinch's St Mary's, Bathwick, was the first serious Gothic Revival church in Bath. Opened in 1820, it is a copy of a typical Somerset late-medieval 'wool church'. The chancel, by G.E. Street, was not added until 1873.

37 H.E. Goodridge was a competent neo-classicist, but his neo-Gothic work left a lot to be desired. This strange church is Holy Trinity, Combe Down, built in 1835.

38 St Saviour's, Larkhall, was built as a result of the Church Building Act of 1824 that helped finance churches in poor areas. The churches are often called 'commissioners' churches'. This one was designed by John Pinch's son, John Pinch the Younger, and opened in 1831. The chancel was added by C.E. Davis in 1882.

39 There is a magnificent, but still not quite finished, mid-nineteenth-century Roman Catholic church in the college at Prior Park, designed in a neo-classical style by Scholes. The main Catholic church in the city is contemporary but completely different. This Gothic Revival church was built by Charles Hansom, brother of the designer of the Hansom cab, and has a spire 222 feet high. It was opened in 1863.

radical rebuilding and enlargement in the 1820s. Another Perpendicular tower survives in the church of St Michael in Twerton, the industrial area to the west of the city. The rest of the church was rebuilt twice in the nineteenth century, but it also boasts a reset Norman doorway.

The remainder of the churches and chapels in Bath are of no great historic interest, but of wide architectural diversity. The older churches were replaced partly because church-going became part of the social round of Beau Nash's Bath. The draughty medieval piles were neither fashionable enough nor sufficiently warm for their congregations. As the new developments spread beyond the walls of the old city, more churches were needed to save the bothersome walk to the existing ones. In most cases these were built by subscription, with all the seats paid for. The more enlightened allowed a few free seats for the poor.

The best of the surviving propriety chapels is the Octagon in Milsom Street, which was renowned in its day. Designed by Thomas Lightoler and opened in 1767, it was tucked away behind the main houses on the street. The name came from its floor plan – an octagonal shape occupying a rectangular building. It boasts a first-floor gallery supported by Ionic columns. Later it became redundant and was used as a showroom. It is now the exhibition hall of the Royal Photographic Society.

At first the prevailing style for the new churches was, inevitably, Palladian. However, less strict neo-classical styles were soon in evidence. By the end of the century fairly serious attempts were being made to revive the medieval Gothic style. This is seen, for instance, in the rather insipid example of John Palmer's Christ Church in Montpelier Row, opened in 1798. John Pinch's St Mary's in Bathwick is better and is a close copy of a Perpendicular Somersetshire 'wool church', opened in 1820. In the main, the later churches were all built in the Gothic Revival style, with varying results.

Nonconformity was surprisingly popular in fashionable Bath, and it wasn't supported by the working classes alone. Lady Huntingdon built and maintained a magnificent chapel off the Vineyards for her own particular brand, or Connection, of Methodism. Designed in the 'Gothick' style and opened in 1765, it was approved of by Horace Walpole, a key figure in the then light-hearted revival of medieval motifs. He wrote that 'The

40 Lady Huntingdon's Connection was an aristocratic form of Methodism started by Selina, Countess of Huntingdon. The chapel, in the Vineyards, was opened for service on 6 October 1767. The bay window in the centre with its Gothick ogee-headed lights belongs to the minister's house, originally built on to the front of the chapel to accommodate visiting preachers. The chapel now belongs to the Bath Preservation Trust and is a museum dedicated to the building of Bath.

41 Walcot Chapel took just over a year to build and was opened in May 1816 (despite the date on the pediment). A fine example of Wesleyan architecture, it was designed by the Revd William Jenkins who built one very similar to this in Lambeth, London, shortly afterwards.

42 The Temperance Movement began in the United States in 1818 and was quickly taken up in Britain. Bath's Temperance Society began in the 1830s and by 1847 it had built this rather austere temperance hall at the bottom of Holloway. It is now a chapel.

Chapel is very neat, with true Gothic windows'. In front of the chapel is a small lodging for either the Countess herself or visiting ministers. It has a full-height battlemented bay boasting Gothick ogee-headed windows. Later a Presbyterian chapel and then a United Reformed church, it came into the hands of the Bath Preservation Trust in 1983 and is now a fascinating museum dedicated to the building of Bath.

The next earliest nonconformist chapel still standing is the former Presbyterian chapel in Trim Street, opened in 1795 and built to the designs of John Palmer. The remaining chapels mostly date from the nineteenth century. The best of these is probably Walcot chapel, a good example of the Wesleyan style of Methodist architecture, opened in 1816 (despite the date on the pediment). It was designed by the Revd William Jenkins, a prolific designer of plain but elegant neo-classical chapels.

44 The old Ebeneezer Chapel, on Pulteney Road in Dolemeads, was built near the bottom lock on the Kennet & Avon canal. It opened in 1821 and shows how Gothic motifs such as pointed arches and battlements could be fitted into a symmetrical, neo-classical façade. It is one of the few chapels still thriving.

Public
Buildings

Bath has a large number of public buildings because of its past life as a centre of healing and fashionable recreation. The earliest were no doubt built by the Romans and for the past two hundred years tantalizing fragments have come to light. A reservoir is known to have been built around the main sacred spring by the construction of high walls around it. Originally open to the sky, a vaulted barrel roof was apparently added at the start of the third century AD. The thrust of the vault proved too great for the walls, so that the north-east corner collapsed and massive buttresses had to be added to stabilize the structure – even Roman architects could get it wrong! The water from the reservoir fed the Great Bath and the smaller bath-houses.

The Great Bath measured 22 metres by nearly 9 metres, and was lined with lead. Originally it had a timber roof supported on a colonnade. It too was then given a vaulted roof of hollow box tiles covered in concrete. This time, however, the piers of the colonnade were thickened to take the the extra weight. After the Romans left, the Great Bath, with the rest of the complex, was left alone and as the mud gradually built up it was forgotten about. Roman finds began appearing in the eighteenth century, but the Great Bath itself was not rediscovered until the 1880s. Restored by the Victorians, the whole complex, deep below the streets of Bath but again open to the sky, looks impressive but little real Roman masonry survives above the pedestals of the columns.

Nothing is left of the medieval baths, as they were all radically rebuilt in the eighteenth century. Only a single archway, possibly

45 The King's Bath was radically restored by C.E. Davies in the 1880s and little survives of anything from before that date. However, it was at least given something of a pre-Georgian style during the rebuilding.

46 John Wood the Younger's Hot Bath was opened in 1778 and is a solid Palladian pile with few decorative fripperies. The portico has plain Doric columns and the cornice is equally austere. Inside, the layout is symmetrical around the octagonal bath itself, with lobbies, dressing rooms and private slip baths as well.

47 There has been a Cross Bath of sorts since at least the start of the fourteenth century and probably for many years before that. The present structure with its lovely, flowing curves was designed by Baldwin in the late 1780s and blends superbly with the end of Bath Street.

47 Detail of neoclassical frieze of the Cross Bath, a ram's head and swags.

47 The inside of Baldwin's Cross Bath was unfortunately ripped out in about 1880.

dating from restoration at the end of the sixteenth century, survives from the pre-Georgian King's Bath. This bath was repeatedly restored, the last major work being undertaken in 1889 by C.E. Davis. The two other surviving baths are the Hot Bath and the Cross Bath. The former, with its Tuscan portico, was designed by Wood the Younger and opened in 1778. Square in plan, it has entrance lobbies on the canted corners that lead to paired dressing rooms. In the centre the octagonal Hot Bath was open to the sky. The nearby Cross Bath shows just how far architectural taste had moved on by the time it was rebuilt in the mid-1780s. The severe masculine Palladianism perpetuated by Wood was replaced by the much gentler, flowing curves of Baldwin, combining both Adamish and Baroque motifs. Sadly, the interior was stripped in about 1880.

Many visitors never bathed, but drank the water instead. It

6 The inside of the Pump Room is a good place for rest and refreshment during any tour around Bath. Usually there is live classical music to help re-create, briefly, the atmosphere of Georgian high society.

48 The New, or Upper, Assembly Rooms were designed by John Wood the Younger after a costlier design by Robert Adam had been rejected. The splendid suite opened in 1771. Their external appearance was not helped by the addition of a new card room to the east of the Octagon in 1777, seen here to the right of the building.

48 A first-floor window of Wood the Younger's New Assembly Room.

48 It is difficult to believe that the fine interior of the New Assembly Rooms was only finished at the start of the 1960s. The original interior was destroyed when the building was badly damaged in the bombing of 1942. This is the former ballroom.

was for these people that the first Pump Room was built in 1706. In 1789 Baldwin began to build a new Great Pump Room, but he was replaced as architect in 1793 by John Palmer, who was largely responsible for the elegant interior. Visitors now mainly drink tea or coffee – the water tastes horrible. John Brydon added the Concert Room in 1894–6 as part of a general improvement scheme connected with the rediscovery of the Roman baths.

The first Assembly Rooms, catering for the fashionable visitors to Bath, were opened in 1708 near the Orange Grove. They became known as the Lower Rooms, but were destroyed by fire in 1820. The growth of the fashionable new Upper Town in the mid-eighteenth century created a demand for new Assembly Rooms in that quarter, and these opened in 1771. Designed by John Wood the Younger and sited between Bennet Street and

48 The elegant tea room of the Assembly Rooms, once the hub of the social life of Georgian Bath.

49 In the days before any form of national health service, the poor relied mostly on charity if they fell ill. Bath had several dispensaries, including this elegant example in Cleveland Place. Designed by Goodridge in 1845, it is basically Palladian but has elements of the Greek Revival. Note the projecting blocks of ashlar on the right-hand side, ready to take the front of an extension that was never built.

50 Opened in 1742, the General Hospital was designed by Wood the Elder. The Palladian proportions of his building were ruined when John Pinch added an attic storey in 1793. More space was provided by a new block further west, completed in 1860 by Manners and Gill, but echoing Wood's original. The hospital is now the Royal Mineral Water Hospital.

51 St Catherine's Hospital, Beau Street, was designed in the neo-Tudor style by George Manners in 1829 and is an early example of the style in the city for a large secular project of this type.

Alfred Street, the New, or Upper, Rooms originally contained a large tea room, a larger ballroom and an octagonal card room. Gutted in 1942, the building was virtually rebuilt by Sir Albert Richardson and reopened in 1963.

Bath also has the more standard public buildings of a city of its size, for the sick, administration, education, pleasure, the poor and the imprisoned.

Not everyone who lived in, or came to, Bath could afford medical treatment, let alone enjoy the delights of the baths. The idea of a hospital to cater for the respectable poor was first mooted at the start of the eighteenth century, but work only started on such a scheme in 1738. Wood designed a standard Palladian front on the lines of a fashionable country house, while Allen provided most of the stone from his own quarries for nothing. The rest of the costs were raised by subscription, and the General

52 The Guildhall was eventually built by Baldwin in the late 1770s. The centrepiece is a fairly standard Palladian exercise, but the rest shows clear signs of being influenced by the work of Robert Adam and the freer neo-classical style.

52 This corner of the Guildhall is by John McKean Brydon and was part of an extension added in 1891. Brydon later worked extensively in London, reintroducing the English Baroque of Wren to the capital.

Hospital opened in Upper Borough Walls in 1742.

The Guildhall on High Street is, architecturally, deceptive as the wings were added well over a century after it had opened. Its foundation stone was laid in 1768, but controversy over the design led to the scheme being halted. In 1776 a completely new design, by Thomas Baldwin, was agreed on. This was clearly influenced by the gentler neo-classicism seen in Pulteney Bridge nearby, which had been opened two years earlier. The interior decoration is exquisitely delicate, and the magnificent first-floor banqueting hall, running the full length of the building, is arguably one of the finest public rooms in England.

Baldwin's Guildhall consisted of the central block flanked by low screens on either side. Towards the end of the nineteenth century more space was needed, so, in 1891, John Brydon demolished the screens and added new two-storey wings.

52 Queen Victoria seldom looked amused in the thousands of statues erected in her honour. This example is in John Brydon's art gallery extension of the Guildhall complex, opened in 1900.

Although clearly echoing elements of the Baroque, the new work respected the old. The ornate cupolas on the corner towers are sufficiently distanced from the central block, which in turn has a tall dome to restore the balance of the composition. Brydon went on to add the art gallery extension between 1898 and 1900. All in all, Brydon showed a degree of sensitivity in these additions all too rare among his, and, indeed, some of our, contemporaries.

The earliest recorded school in Bath was founded in 1552 and funded by monastery lands given to the city by Edward VI. The Free Grammar School of King Edward VI had an eventful life, and at the start of the eighteenth century occupied the nave of the disused church of St Mary's. Prisoners were housed in the tower! A new school was designed by Thomas Jelly in Broad Street and was opened in 1752.

There were once several theatres in Bath to which its

53 King Edward's Grammar School on Broad Street was designed by Thomas Jelly on the site of the Black Swan Inn. Jelly designed relatively few houses in Bath which, judging from the quality of this Palladian façade, is a pity.

54 The rather forbidding front of Kingswood School faces Lansdown Road. The school was founded by John Wesley in Bristol to teach the sons of Methodist preachers, but moved to Bath in 1852. The neo-Tudor buildings are by Wilson, who also built St Swithin's almshouses, not far away, in 1842.

55 The Theatre Royal is still best seen from Beaufort Square, as in this photograph. In comparison with Dance's elegant neo-classical façade of 1805, the present entrance in the Sawclose looks exactly what it is – a rather inelegant afterthought.

Georgian visitors could go to watch some of the best 'turns' of the age. Only two survive and just one of these is still in use. The Orchard Street Theatre was started by Thomas Jelly in 1749 and rebuilt internally by John Palmer in 1775. From the outside it looks no different from the houses next to it. It closed in 1805 and now serves as the freemasons' hall. The Theatre Royal in Beaufort Square opened in 1805 and was designed by George Dance. Its grand front is highly original, with panelled pilasters supporting a heavily garlanded frieze. After the theatre was gutted by fire in 1862 it was rebuilt. For some reason, the new entrance was on the Sawclose, a rather untidy affair tacked on to early eighteenth-century houses.

56 This former theatre in the Sawclose was built at the end of the nineteenth century, opposite the new entrance to the Theatre Royal. Known previously as the Regency, and the Palace, it closed in 1965 and is now a bingo hall. Its architecture may not be 'classic', but it certainly is full of life.

Houses

Before the 1720s, and after the 1820s, the houses of Bath were very little different from those in any other town of similar size in the region. In the hundred years between, however, the city saw the construction of some of the finest and most influential, high-class urban housing in the country. So successful was Bath in the eighteenth century that little survives of anything built before this time.

The oldest house in Bath is said to be Sally Lunn's House on North Parade Passage, which is reputed to date back to 1482. The front is certainly much later and was probably remodelled in the early eighteenth century. Abbey Church House, although substantially rebuilt after being badly damaged in the bombing of 1942, gives a much better impression of a typical house of late sixteenth-century Bath. Built in about 1570, its name changed often over the years. From the late eighteenth century it was known as Hetling House before being bought and restored by the abbey in the 1880s.

At the start of the eighteenth century houses were still generally built individually. The taste for classical symmetry was more and more evident, as sash windows replaced mullioned casements, ashlar replaced rubblestone and classical mouldings appeared; but dormer gables persisted. This type of house can still be seen in some parts of the centre, particularly in Broad Street and Chapel Court.

Two pre-Wood houses, whose architects are unknown, illustrate how Bath may have continued to develop its own brand of provincial Palladianism. Trim Street was begun in 1707 and was the first major development outside the old city. The best surviving house is No. 5, known as 'General Wolfe's House', and probably built shortly before 1720. The centre of its five-bay façade is given due prominence by fluted pilasters, which are Ionic on

57 Sally Lunn's House, on the left of the two gabled houses is said to date back to the fifteenth century, but has certainly been rebuilt on several occasion. Its street face is typical of the very early eighteenth century. Sally was a seventeenth century cake-seller trading in what was then called Lilliput Alley. Its modern name, North Parade Passage, is not an improvement.

58 Abbey Church House, known for many years as Hetling House, dates back to about 1570. Altered frequently over the years by its different owners, it came into the hands of Bath Abbey in 1888. Severely damaged in the bombing of 1942, it was painstakingly restored and now stands as a rare example of Bath's early domestic architecture.

59 Tucked away in Church Lane near the medieval centre of Widcombe village is a house that probably dates back to the seventeenth century. Built mainly of rubblestone, it has later ashlar extensions and most of the upper portion has been rendered.

60 No. 5 Trim Street is known as 'General Wolfe's House' and was built in about 1720 as a good example of pre-Wood provincial Palladianism. The centre bay is given prominence in a symmetrical façade and the roof is hidden.

the ground floor and Corinthian above, supporting segmental heads to the front door and the first-floor window. The roof is hidden behind a parapet.

Another general, General Wade, lived at the house in Abbey Church Yard that now bears his name. Although built at about the same time as the house in Trim Street it shows a far more sophisticated brand of Palladianism. Its fluted Ionic pilasters are of the 'giant order' – that is they rise through more than just one storey – and this is the first use of this motif in Bath. Oddly, the building is of four bays, which means that there is an odd number of pilasters. In classical architecture there should, strictly, always be an even number.

To create his new Bath, Wood had to design on a much bigger scale. Large urban schemes were not new. Neither was the notion of grand squares of high-class housing, several having already been laid out in France. Inigo Jones created the first

61 Roughly contemporary with 'General Wolfe's House' in Trim Street is 'General Wade's House' in the Abbey Church Yard. The Palladian design is better and more adventurous, but the architect is unknown. The Ionic pilasters are the first in Bath of the 'giant order', rising through two storeys. The effect would have been better before the present Regency shop-front was added.

62 Beau Nash moved from one house in the Sawclose to one virtually next door. Both were designed by a local stonemason, Thomas Greenway. The house where Nash spent the last years of his life was probably built in the 1720s and is unusual for central Bath in being detached. It also has its entrance on the end, rather than in the longer, more imposing elevation.

English piazza at Covent Garden in the early seventeenth century. Later on a series of such squares was created in London, but around them the owners of the individual houses built to their own individual style.

This wasn't good enough for Wood, so he set about a new way of doing things. He took calculated risks on a big scale. First he designed the general layout of a new development and the street façades of the houses. Then he leased the land needed. The individual building plots in the scheme were then sub-leased, at a profit, to other builders. They built the houses on the understanding that they would make sure that the design of the façade was respected. This meant that Wood often had little to do with the layout of the houses behind the frontages, which were built to individual requirements, a fact readily appreciated from the back of even the best developments.

63 Ralph Allen's town house was near the Abbey in Lilliput Alley, and in 1727 a new extension was added. This once overlooked a large garden and from it Allen could have seen his Sham Castle on Claverton Down. Now it is tucked away in a narrow alley. Palladian in style, though rather over-decorated, it has been attributed to Wood.

64 Wood designed the portion of Gay Street between Old King Street and George Street in the mid-1730s and, twenty years later, extended the street northwards to his proposed Circus. The three-storey houses are fairly plain, except for the corner building with its ornate full-height corner bow. This was finished by 1736 for a rich Quaker and is an eye-catcher on the north-east corner of Queen Square.

65 Kingsmead Square was laid out by John Strahan shortly after Wood had started Queen Square. It is really only an open space originally surrounded by well-proportioned, but fairly simply decorated, three-storey terraces. It lacks the feel for townscape demonstrated by Wood in Queen Square.

19 A typically solid and well-crafted door by Strahan, in Beauford Square.

66 A tripartite window, combining classical proportions with Gothick detail in the glazing bars of the middle sashes, seems to have been very fashionable in late eighteenth-century Bath. This particular example is in London Street.

Wood's first grand scheme was Queen Square, begun in 1728 and virtually finished by 1736. Built on the slopes north of the old city it was designed to look like a noble courtyard and in Wood's words, 'soars above the other Buildings with a Sprightliness, which gives it the Elegance and Grandeur of the Body of a stately Palace'. The north range of seven large houses was the 'palace' itself and was treated accordingly. The central five bays are accentuated by a portico, and the three bays at either end break slightly forward as well to appear as pavilions. The portico and pavilions are given attached, three-quarter Corinthian columns and the sections between have matching pilasters. The rest of the buildings around the square were designed to be foils to the main range and, from his own home in the central house of the south terrace, Wood could admire, and show off to guests, his pioneering composition.

(*text continues on p. 84*)

67 Rosewell House in Kingsmead Square is a rare and very late example of provincial Baroque, built in 1736 for Thomas Rosewell. It has been attributed to John Strahan, who laid out the square and the nearby streets, but is quite different from anything else he is known to have designed in the city.

68 Prior Park, the magnificent Palladian mansion John Wood designed for Ralph Allen in the late 1730s, was gutted by fire for the second time in 1991. Some idea of the quality of the building can be seen in this Palladian lodge, built at around the same time. This was Lower Lodge and the gate pier to the right was part of a gateway to the main drive to the house, a private road until the 1930s. Widcombe village lies along the lane to the left.

69 A section of John Wood's posthumous masterpiece, the Circus, part of an ambitious plan to re-create in Bath the grandeur of Imperial Rome. The circular plan means that there is no beginning or end to the design and it is just punctuated by three streets leading from it. Four streets would have ruined the effect.

70 Milsom Street was laid out in the early 1760s for residential housing of a standard, simplified, Palladian design. As it was situated between the old city and the new Upper Town, it quickly became the most fashionable of shopping streets, which it still is.

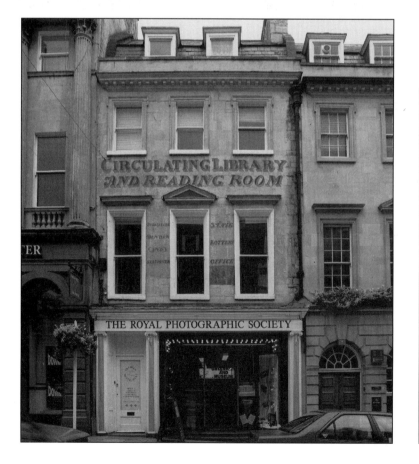

71 This is a typical terraced house of the 1760s in Milsom Street, built to designs submitted by John Horton. Plain Palladian in character with standard detailing, including a pedimented central first-floor window, it is of a type built in large numbers in Bath. The preserved sign-writing on the masonry gives this house additional interest, as does the fact that behind it is the Octagon, the former chapel opened in 1767 and now an exhibition gallery for the Royal Photographic Society.

15 The dramatic sweep of the Royal Crescent shows that the younger Wood had as good an eye for grand architectural gestures as his father. He only designed the front wall; the rest was built as individual houses by individual builders for individual clients. This first crescent, begun in 1767, was widely copied throughout Britain.

15 The Royal Crescent, unlike the elder Wood's Circus, is not lavishly ornate. It relies purely on proportion and position for effect, and the relentless march of the giant order of attached Ionic columns along the façade.

This idea was soon copied, and by the 1730s Strahan was laying out Beaufort and Kingsmead Squares to the west. These lack any of Wood's sense of grandeur, and simply consist of worthy terraces of more or less uniform houses around small open spaces. Similar terraces were built along streets, old and new. Wood's next major urban housing project concerned his Forum, but only the North and South Parades were ever completed. Begun in 1740, these were robbed of much of the rich decoration that Wood had planned for them.

Wood's two masterpieces were very different. For Ralph Allen he designed Prior Park, a mansion built above Widcombe and overlooking the city. Started in 1734 and almost finished by 1742, it has been described as one of the finest Palladian mansions in Britain. Wood's design was changed during construction and its symmetry lost. Subsequently the wings have been altered

73 The uniformity of Milsom Street was relieved in 1782 by the construction of Somersetshire Buildings. Designed by Thomas Baldwin, they originally consisted of five houses in a bold, symmetrical group – arguably one of the architect's best works. The design veers away from Palladianism towards the less restricted neo-classicism of Robert Adam and his followers, and the decoration of some of the window surrounds is extremely delicate.

12 Camden Crescent was designed by John Eveleigh and work started in 1788. It was to rival the Royal Crescent in the quality of its architecture and in its superb hillside position. Unfortunately, the ground was unstable and the eastern part was never finished. Despite its unbalanced look, with only a truncated section to the right of the 'central' portico, it is still one of the best terraces in Bath.

12 The centrepiece of Eveleigh's Camden Crescent is this attached portico. Technically, it is wrong. Classical porticoes have an even number of columns, while this one has five. Visually, the column in the middle creates the illusion of pushing up the middle of the pediment.

and added to as part of a Roman Catholic college that has occupied the site, on and off, since the 1830s. The main house has also been gutted twice by fire, the last time being in 1991. It is now being restored.

In complete contrast, Wood finally managed to begin work on his Circus in the Upper Town, just north of Queen Square. The foundation stone was laid in February 1754, but he died within a few months of this. The Circus was, and is, a remarkable achievement. The three separate segments, containing thirty-three houses in all, were separated by streets leading the eye to very different vistas. Smollett's Squire Bramble wrote, 'The Circus is a pretty bauble; contrived for shew, and looks like Vespasian's amphitheatre turned outside in'. The Roman influence is obvious and the decoration lavish, with separate orders of columns on each of the three main floors. These are

74 Bath Street is one of the few to be built by the corporation. It was begun in 1791 and designed by Baldwin. With colonnades down both sides, it provided a covered walk between the Hot and Cross Baths at one end, and the Pump Room and other baths off Stall Street at the other. At each end the buildings open out into a semicircle, a detail particularly effective next to the sinuous Cross Bath.

75 A detail of one of the houses in Laura Place. It has kept all its original sashes, door, and elegant throwover and ironwork.

'superimposed' in their classically correct places, with Doric on the ground floor, Ionic on the second and Corinthian at the top. The wide variety of motifs carved in the friezes is well worth study. As the houses are arranged in a circle there is no central feature to detract from a continuous architectural pattern.

The last great original gesture in Bath was the younger Wood's Royal Crescent, built at the end of one of the streets leading from the Circus. Started in 1767, it contains thirty houses originally on the edge of the city and overlooking it. Its windy and somewhat isolated position was ridiculed at the time by the caricaturist Rowlandson, among others. It is far plainer than the Circus, the only real decoration being the giant order of attached three-quarter Ionic columns, 114 in all, marking each bay. Even the centre of the crescent is very underplayed – just paired columns flanking the central windows. The crescent idea was

76 The architect of Marlborough Buildings is unknown, but they are generally considered to be the work of Palmer or Baldwin. Built in about 1790, they helped to protect the Royal Crescent from the wind blowing in from the west.

77 The central feature of John Eveleigh's Somerset Place is unique in Bath, being topped by a bold, broken, segmental pediment. Built in about 1791, the crescent continues the sinuous line along the contour begun by Palmer's contemporary Lansdown Crescent to the east. Badly damaged in the 1942 bombing, Somerset Place has been carefully restored.

78 Eveleigh designed a huge development well outside the city on the London Road in the early 1790s. The centrepiece, literally, was to be the Grosvenor Hotel with its audacious six-bay façade with garlanded Ionic columns – a mixture of Palladianism and bad taste. The scheme, ambitious from the start, fell victim to the 1793 crash and the buildings were not finished until the 1820s. Some of the decorative carving is still incomplete. The proposed hotel became part of a college.

copied several more times in Bath and became popular in many towns and cities throughout England, but none can match this prototype.

All the time other architects and speculators were adding new streets to cater for the growing needs of the city. Often the construction of the buildings left a lot to be desired. Some of the partition walls, for example, are extremely thin – often made of ashlar blocks as little as 6 inches wide. In the 1760s Squire Bramble was convinced that any reasonably strong man could 'push his foot through the strongest part of their walls'.

Towards the end of the eighteenth century, and into the early decades of the nineteenth, houses continued to be built largely in terraces or crescents as part of more or less grand schemes. Such was the demand for accommodation that they were often built at some distance from the city centre and well into what

78 Detail of windows in Grosvenor Place, showing a typical Eveleigh mask.

79 Widcombe Crescent is somewhat austere, stripped of any unnecessary ostentation and probably designed by Charles Harcourt Masters. Built around 1805, it consists of fourteen houses, but is designed to look as though there are fewer, grander houses. The doorways to adjacent houses share a single, round-arched recess, and above them the central part of the tripartite window on the dividing walls is blank. The string courses and windows of the six central houses are just slightly higher than those on either side.

had been countryside. The neo-classical decoration made popular by Adam tended to be far subtler than the Palladian, but in some cases almost too subtle for the size of the terraces. Nevertheless, even those built in the 1820s are fine examples of urban planning and refinement. Large numbers were built as lodging houses and were only later adapted as family homes. In the latter part of the eighteenth century, and throughout the nineteenth, the ground floors of many houses in the city centre became shops and were altered accordingly.

The basic concepts used in middle- and upper-class housing were also used, in suitably humbler form, for the lower classes. Streets of two- or three-storey terraces on the edge of the more fashionable quarters housed the artisans needed to service the city or work on its industries. Too few have survived and some of those that have are still threatened. Two of the terraces that

13 John Pinch designed several plain but elegant terraces around the city in the early years of the nineteenth century, each having to cope with a different type of site. The eleven houses of New Sydney Place have to climb a gentle slope, so Pinch stepped the houses and their architectural features accordingly, while still retaining the overall unity of the terrace. The full-height terminal bow windows were one of his trademarks.

80 High on the hillside overlooking Bath, Sion Hill Place was quite out in the country when built and some distance from the next houses. The restrained dignity of the design is typical of John Pinch. The terrace was built between 1818 and 1820, and retains much of its privacy and seclusion.

81 Prior Park Buildings, built in the mid-1820s, are nicely set back on a private lane separated from busy Prior Park Road by gardens and a canalized stream. Usually attributed to John Pinch, this was one of the last of the great terraces of Bath to be built. The refinement seen in his other buildings is here compromised by the door and window pattern of the ground floor, and the peculiar attic over the central pediment. Perhaps Pinch's plans were altered during building or later.

82 Ralph Allen was, for the times, a far-sighted employer and realized that providing fine housing was one way of keeping good staff. He built two ranges of plain but quality houses for his employees, this one of three storeys being near the bottom of the inclined railway and close to the quay. Known as Ralph Allen's Cottages they were almost demolished in the bleak days of early 1970s redevelopments.

Ralph Allen built for his workers to designs by Wood still stand. Ralph Allen Cottages, at the bottom of Ralph Allen Drive near to Dolemeads Quay, and the terrace near the stone mines on Combe Down, two miles away, are early examples of good-quality industrial housing.

Such was the success of the grand terrace in Bath that it is easy to overlook the few individual houses of quality that were built during the Georgian period. Prior Park has already been mentioned, and its former lodges are, in themselves, very good Palladian houses in miniature. Not far from Prior Park is Widcombe Manor, rebuilt in about 1727 to the design of an unknown architect, but one well versed in the latest contemporary fashions. Another important Georgian house, though much later, is Doric House, Sion Hill, an early example of the Greek Revival style built in 1803–5.

(*text continues on p. 102*)

83 Widcombe Manor was rebuilt in about 1727 in a loose Palladian style not seen elsewhere in Bath. Its façade has definite elements of the English Baroque and in some ways echoes John Vanbrugh's house at Kings Weston, near Bristol, begun in about 1710. The architect is unknown.

84 The aptly named Doric House on Sion Hill is one of Bath's often overlooked architectural treasures. This unique house, built in about 1810, is an early example of the purist Greek Revival style. It was built for the painter Thomas Barker, and is part house and part art gallery. The architect was Joseph Michael Gandy, better known for his books and drawings on architecture than for his buildings.

85 Bath's architecture is generally renowned for its restraint and elegance, so this house in Victoria Park is totally out of character, but great fun! The *cottage ornée* was part of the fashion for the 'antique rustic' look in the early nineteenth century. This gardener's cottage is quasi-Tudor, with ridiculous bargeboards. It was probably designed in about 1830 by Edward Davis, who was responsible for the nearby park gates.

86 The early nineteenth-century Gothic Cottage on Sion Hill is not only unusual because of its design, but also because of its brickwork. Brick was not a common building material in Bath and never has been.

87 The terrace went out of fashion in the middle and upper classes in the Victorian period, and was replaced by the detached house and the typical English compromise – the semi-detached. This rather magnificent pair of nineteenth-century 'semis' is in Henrietta Street, part of Baldwin's unfinished Bathwick project. Designed to look like one house, the central windows are blank.

88 Not all modern housing is bad. The post-modernist architecture of today can only really be judged by posterity, but at least it offers interesting shapes on a more human scale than the high-rise square blocks of the 1960s and 1970s. This is part of a new residential development off Walcot Road, tucked away out of the main skyline of the city.

The grand terraced house went out of fashion in Victorian times as privacy became more and more important. There was, instead, a demand for detached houses in the suburbs, and also the growth of the ubiquitous English 'semi'. Examples of both can be seen all around Bath. The terraced house became more or less confined to the lower classes, no longer with any architectural pretensions.

Industrial Buildings and Bridges

Bath is not a city generally associated with industry, so it may come as a surprise to find that it has had an important industrial economy since the medieval period. Perhaps one of its oldest industries is stone quarrying, which was begun by the Romans. The ease with which the stone could be cut and carved made it very popular, and it is known to have been used at some distance from the quarries in the Saxon period. At the start of the eighteenth century Ralph Allen radically increased the output of the quarries on and below Combe Down, but there are few obvious traces of this activity above ground.

As part of his improvements, Allen built one of the very first railways in the south of England. His 'carriageway' was a long, inclined plane running down from Combe Down to the Dolemead Wharfs on the newly improved Avon, and was probably opened in 1732. Today the steady gradient of Ralph Allen Drive, leading up to Prior Park, more or less reflects the route of this long-abandoned line. The legacy of Bath's stone industry is beginning to cause concern. From the Georgian period the stone blocks were usually mined, rather than quarried, often from great depths below the ground. Recently the man-made subterranean passageways and caverns under Combe Down have shown signs of collapse and solutions are urgently needed to prevent subsidence in the later suburbs built above the old stone mines.

20 Pulteney Bridge is one of the most elegant of bridges and was designed by Robert Adam. It is said to reflect Palladio's proposal for the Rialto Bridge in Venice, but the connection is rather tenuous – that scheme was far more elaborate. Nevertheless, the Italian influence is obvious. The bridge was built between 1769 and 1774.

20 The road-level view of Pulteney bridge gives no clues that it actually is a bridge. The street is lined by small shops, the domed buildings being the tollhouses. Because the shops are so small, over the years additions were made to them on both sides, jutting out over the river and disfiguring the bridge. All those on the downstream side have now been removed.

89 The North Parade Bridge was built in 1936, replacing one of 1836. It is still a graceful structure.

Apart from its stone and its springs, Bath's other main natural resource was the River Avon. In the medieval period any river with a fast and reliable flow was an obvious source of water power. Weirs thrown across the river harnessed the current and directed it to waterwheels. The weir below Pulteney Bridge was remodelled as late as 1971, but there has probably been a weir on the site for a thousand years or more. For many centuries it served mills on either bank. These were used originally for grinding corn or other cereals, but later for other purposes. In the West Country a flourishing woollen industry grew up from the thirteenth century onwards, and a special type of mill, the fulling mill, was developed to work the woven cloth. Several of these are known to have existed in the Bath reach of the river, but there are no significant traces of the city's medieval weaving industry left.

In 1728 the Avon was navigable as far upstream as Bath, providing the city with an important link with the port of Bristol. Despite several careful plans, the next major improvement in the city's transport links had to wait until the start of the nineteenth century. Authorized in 1794, the Kennet & Avon canal was finally completed in 1810. It joined the Avon at Bath with the Kennet at Newbury, providing the final link in a waterway between Bristol and London. It was built as a 'broad' canal, capable of taking boats twice as wide as the typical 'narrow' boats. Engineered by John Rennie, it boasts some splendid structures, notably the Dundas Aqueduct over the Avon a few miles upstream of the city.

In Bath itself, the canal is notable for the polite way it passes by. A gently spaced flight of locks rises from the Avon at Widcombe, then the canal skirts the southern edge of the city.

90 This ornate archway is merely a bridge carrying pipes to a nearby laundry and was designed by C.E. Davis. Built at the end of the 1880s it was part of a general tidying up in this area ,connected with the newly discovered Roman baths. The Queen's Bath stood on the right, but was destroyed in order to allow the Roman Great Bath to be displayed.

91 In Bath, even industrial architecture can be graceful. These cast-iron bridges reflected in the Kennet and Avon canal are in Sydney Gardens and are dated to 1800. In 1801 Jane Austen wrote from Bath: 'Last night we walked by the Canal', but it was not until nine years later that the canal was finally linked with the river.

92 This rather delightful Gothick lock-keeper's cottage sits beside the top lock of the Widcombe flight, and there are good views of the city from the towpath on this stretch of the canal.

93 Cleveland House, the former offices of the canal company, was built over a short tunnel taking the canal under Sydney Road and into the Gardens. This is the back view. At this point the towpath changes from the right-hand side to the left, on a 'roving bridge' immediately in front of the tunnel.

Elegant stone and cast-iron bridges cross over it as it wends through Sydney Gardens, enhancing, rather than detracting from, the scene. A walk along the quiet canal bank, hidden for the most part from the city's bustle, is a pleasant excursion. The present condition of the canal is a tribute to many years of voluntary hard work and dedication. In 1951, after decades of neglect, it was officially declared unnavigable, but British Waterways' plea for the canal to be abandoned was, fortunately, turned down. Later a Kennet & Avon Canal Assocation began to plan its restoration – a dream finally realized in 1976.

Brunel's Great Western Railway, like the canal, was built to a 'broad' gauge – in this case one of 7 feet – but eventually lost the 'Battle of the Gauges' and had to be converted to the standard gauge. Trains began running from Bath to Bristol in 1840, and to London in the following year. The GWR's architectural

95 Railways by their very nature cannot be as tranquil as canals, but at least the Great Western Railway treated Sydney Gardens with some respect. The quality of the ashlar retaining walls is impeccable and the company even provided a balustraded walk alongside the tracks.

96 Green Park Station was opened as the Midland Railway's Queen Square station in 1869. Threatened with demolition after it finally closed in 1966, it has recently been restored as part of a new supermarket complex. It is an excellent example of saving redundant buildings by generating new uses for them.

style was mainly Tudor Gothic, even down to the minor accommodation bridges with their pointed arches. The GWR station, now Bath Spa, was built in the vaguely neo-Jacobean style of I.K. Brunel, quite alien to the architecture of the city it served. Nearby the lines are carried over the roads by castellated Gothic bridges. Like the canal before it, the GWR had to negotiate Sydney Gardens, and here the company toned down their house style.

The other railway to reach the central part of the city came much later, but its appearance was far more in keeping. The Midland Railway built a competing route from Bristol to Bath on the opposite side of the Avon and opened a terminus called Queen Square in 1869. The Somerset & Dorset company shared the station from 1874 and it was renamed Green Park in 1951. Its polite Palladian facade by J.H. Sanders hides a fine iron train

97 J.S. Crossley's fine train shed was plain but effective, a symbol of the modern technology of the day. It was hidden behind Sander's Palladian façade, which paid homage to the Bath of the nineteenth century.

shed, with a main roof span of 66 feet designed by J.S. Crossley. Services stopped in 1966 and the station became a rather run-down car park. However, in an encouraging partnership between planners and a supermarket chain, the buildings have been reno-vated in a good example of 'adaptive reuse'. Remains of the former Somerset & Dorset's steep and sinuous route to Evercreech, including two long tunnels, can be traced in the southern suburbs.

With a good transport system firmly established, Bath developed more industries in the nineteenth century. The largest of these still in business is the engineering firm of Stothert and Pitt. Begun as an iron foundry in 1785 by George Stothert, it provided some of the cast-iron footbridges for the Kennet & Avon canal. In 1857 the company moved to the Newark Foundry on Lower Bristol Road, then later became famed for its cranes

and heavy lifting gear. The company has now moved to new premises, the Victoria Works. Other industries in recent years have included corset-making, malting, paper-making and furniture-making, as well as all the normal service industries connected with all cities.

98 Baird's Maltings was built alongside the Kennet & Avon canal, not far from the top lock of the Widcombe flight. It was a typical small maltings, the curious shaped section on the right being the malting kiln itself. Closed in 1972, it became an architect's office and, more recently, a private house.

Follies

In a city given over for so long to recreation and frivolity, it is not too surprising to find one or two surviving follies, those fascinating architectural peccadilloes. The two most prolific folly builders lived on opposite sides of the valley and could not have been less alike in character. Ralph Allen, superficially utilitarian and rather sombre, was in fact a genial host to many a writer and artist, and Pope and Fielding were regular visitors to his mansion at Prior Park. Perhaps it was from these creative men that he got the ideas to enrich the natural beauty of his estate with architectural ornaments. Many have been demolished, but the remnants of a grotto and a sham Roman bridge remain. Near the bottom of the combe is a fine Palladian bridge. This was built by Richard Jones in about 1755, but the design is one of several close copies of the Palladian bridge at Wilton, built in 1736.

Allen's main folly is even more surprising. High on what was then the bare slope of Bathwick Hill, Claverton Down, he built the Sham Castle in about 1762. It was based on an earlier design by Sanderson Miller, a wealthy amateur architect who specialized in designing Rococo Gothic eye-catchers, and it was built by Jones. The 'castle' – a Georgian stage setting in stone – has deliberately overblown 'medieval' details and is only two-dimensional, a single 100 feet long wall with 'towers'. It could originally be seen from Ralph Allen's townhouse in Lilliput Alley, but gradually houses and trees have encroached upon it.

On the opposite slopes was the mile-long, but rather narrow, garden of the most notorious folly builder of all, the eccentric William Beckford. His astonishing Fonthill Abbey in Wiltshire had the tallest spire in England, but fell down. Shortly before, in 1822, partially ruined by its cost and running from scandal, Beckford moved to Bath. Between 1825 and 1838 on the land leading up from Lansdown Crescent to the top of Lansdown

99 Ralph Allen's 'Gothick' Sham Castle once dominated Bathwick Hill and it offered an eye-catching sight from his town house. Now trees and houses have encroached upon it. Attributed to an amateaur folly designer, Sanderson Miller, it was probably built in around 1762.

100 William Beckford was a notorious eccentric who retreated to Bath towards the end of his eventful life. Beckford's Tower on the top of Lansdown Hill was reached by a scenic pathway winding up a long but fairly narrow garden from Beckford's house in Lansdown Crescent. It was designed by Goodridge and finished in 1827.

Hill, he laid out a route full of little surprises, such as an embattled gateway and an Islamic pavilion. It led to the 154 foot high Beckford's Tower – minute by Fonthill standards – built by Goodrich and completed by 1827. Architecturally, it is perhaps best politely described as 'different' – a mixture of Greek and Roman styles with a hint of the Italianate. After Beckford's death it had a mixed career, but is now in private hands and open in the summer.

Further Reading

Local Books

Dallimore, K., *Exploring Bath: 1 Centre and West* (1984)
——, *Exploring Bath: 2 Centre and East* (1986)
Ferguson, A., *The Sack of Bath* (1973)
Haddon, J., *Portrait of Bath* (1982)
Hamilton, M., *Bath Before Beau Nash* (1978)
Ison, W., *The Georgian Buildings of Bath* 2nd ed (1980)
Jackson, N., *Nineteenth Century Bath: Architects and Architecture* (1991)
Mowl, T. and Earnshaw, B., *John Wood: Architect of Obsession* (1988)

General Books

Clifton-Taylor, A., *The Pattern of English Building* (4th ed 1987)
Cossons, N., *The BP Book of Industrial Archaeology* (1987)
Cruickshank, D., *A Guide to the Georgian Buildings of Britain and Ireland.* (1985)
Pevsner, N., *The Buildings of England* series, in county volumes
Summerson, J., *Architecture in Britain 1530–1830* (1989)

Index

Page numbers in bold indicate illustrations.